WiderWorld

POWERED BY

Practice
Tests Plus

EXAM PRACTICE

PEARSON TEST OF ENGLISH GENERAL **LEVEL A1**

Pearson Education Limited
Edinburgh Gate
Harlow
Essex CM20 2JE
and Associated Companies throughout the world.

First published 2016
Sixth Impression 2020
ISBN: 978 1 292 14883 0

Set in Arial
Printed and bound in Great Britain by Ashford Colour Press Ltd

Acknowledgements:
Material for Test 1 from authentic PTE General past papers
Material for Test 2 from *PTE General Skills Practice Level A1*, with revisions

The publisher would like to thank the following for their kind permission to reproduce their images:

(Key: b-bottom; c-centre; l-left; r-right; t-top)

Fotolia.com: 9comeback 33bc, artisticco 40, 60, Matthew Cole 26bc, eceseven 33tl, Gstudio Group 33tc, Stoyan Haytov 26c, Andrey Kokidko 33br, macrovector 26br, pinipin 26bl, pixelalex 26cr, Rzoog 33bl, Klara Viskova 33tr

Illustrations by **Katerina Milusheva**: 6b, 7b, 14, 15b, 26tc, 27b, 32, 34, 46; Jerzy Dołżyk, 24c; Maciej Ufnalewski: 25b

All other images © Pearson Education

Contents

There is no **Section 11** in PTE General Level A1.

Introduction

What is Pearson Test of English General?

PTE General is a suite of six tests at different levels (A1, 1, 2, 3, 4 and 5). It tests your ability in English in practical skills for real-life situations such as writing messages, understanding talks, understanding newspaper and magazine articles or taking part in conversations. PTE General tests are taken three times a year in May, June, and December in centres all around the world.

The tests do not assume any experience of work or knowledge of the world and so are most suitable for teenagers and young adults who expect to use English in their future academic and professional lives.

Key Features

The sections and items in PTE General Level A1 are grouped together into themes or topics related to familiar and routine matters such as the home, the family, work, shopping, education, travel and entertainment. The listening and reading texts are specially written so that the level sounds authentic. The four skills – listening, speaking, reading and writing – are tested in an integrated way. For example, you listen to some information and write about what you have heard, or you read a text, and then answer questions or complete notes based on what you have read.

Test Structure

PTE General is divided into two parts – the Written Test and the Spoken Test.

The Written Test

The Written Test of PTE General consists of nine sections and takes 1 hour and 15 minutes at Level A1.

Section 1: Listening

Section 1 consists of ten short listening texts which are all monologues. Each text is followed by a question and three possible picture options. You must choose the correct answer by putting a cross (✗) in a box. There is a short pause before each recording for you to look at the pictures before you listen, and another pause after the recording for you to choose which of the three pictures matches what you have heard. This section tests your ability to understand the main idea of what someone says. You will hear the recording only once.

Section 2: Listening and Writing

Section 2 is a dictation. You will hear one person speaking and you must write down exactly what you hear with the correct spelling. You will hear the recording twice, the second time with pauses to give you time to write. The recording can be a news broadcast, an announcement, instructions or factual information.

Section 3: Listening

In Section 3, you will hear two listening texts, including announcements and recorded messages. You have to complete notes for each listening using the information you have heard. There are five gaps to fill for each listening text. This section may test your ability to understand and write down detailed information including addresses, telephone numbers and website addresses. You will hear each text twice.

Section 4: Reading

In Section 4, you read five short texts, each containing a gap, and you choose which of three possible answers is the missing word or phrase that fills the gap. This section tests your ability to understand specific information and/or the overall meaning of the text. The reading texts can be instructions, signs, notices, labels, advertisements, menus or announcements.

Section 5: Reading

In Section 5, you read five short texts and for each one you choose one picture which matches the text from a choice of three. This section tests your understanding of the main idea of a text. The reading texts can give descriptions or directions, and the pictures can include maps or diagrams.

Section 6: Reading

There are two reading texts in this section. Each text is followed by four questions for you to answer using a word or a short phrase. They test your understanding of the main points of the texts. The types of reading can be letters, emails, articles from newspapers or magazines, leaflets, brochures or website articles.

Section 7: Reading

In Section 7, you read a text and use the information to fill in seven gaps in sentences or a set of notes. This section tests your understanding of specific detailed information you have read. The reading text can be an email, letter, advertisement, newspaper or magazine article, or a section from a website or textbook.

Section 8: Writing

Section 8 is a writing test. You have to write a piece of correspondence – an email, a formal or an informal letter, a postcard or notes – based on the information that you have read in Section 7. At Level A1, you have to write 30–50 words.

Section 9: Writing

In Section 9, you will be asked to write a text based on a picture. There are two pictures to choose from. The text to write at Level A1 is 50–80 words long. You will be asked to write a short story, a description or a diary entry.

The Spoken Test

The Spoken Test of PTE General consists of three sections (Sections 10, 12 and 13) and takes 5 minutes at Level A1.

Section 10: Speaking

In the first part of the Test, the examiner will ask you a question and you have to talk about yourself for about a minute. You will talk about your interests and hobbies, the sports you take part in, the films or books you like, etc. The examiner may ask you further questions to find out more information.

Section 11

There is no discussion section at Level A1.

Section 12: Speaking

In Section 12, you will be shown a picture and asked to describe it. You will be asked to describe people, interiors (for example, a home, a school, a shop, a restaurant), public places (for example, a street or a park) and everyday activities. You will have about 2 minutes to do this.

Section 13: Speaking

The final section of the Spoken Test is a role play. You will be given a card with details of your role and some instructions. The role play includes situations such as shopping, ordering food and drink, public transportation and asking for directions. This section of the test takes about 1.5 minutes.

Exam Practice: PTE General

The *Exam Practice: PTE General* series has been specially written to help you become familiar with the format and content of the PTE General Test. They contain two full practice tests, plus exam and writing guide sections to help you to improve your general level of English, as well as your score in the test. Level A1 contains:

- Two *Practice Tests* for both the Written and Spoken Tests, the first of which has tips giving advice on how to deal with specific questions, or aspects of questions.

- An *Exam Guide* with advice on how to approach each section and deal with particular problems that might occur.

- A *Writing Guide* which concentrates on the writing tasks you will meet in the tests, giving example answers, writing tips and useful language.

Practice Test 1 with Guidance

Section 1

You will have 10 seconds to read each question. Listen and put a cross (✗) in the box next to the correct answer, as in the example. You have 10 seconds to choose the correct option.

Example: Which table does the woman want?

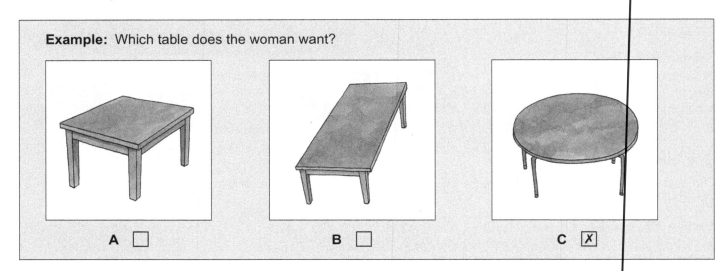

A ☐   B ☐   C ☒

1. Which hotel is the man speaking about?

  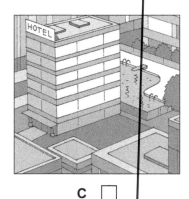

A ☐   B ☐   C ☐

2. Which is the bathroom door?

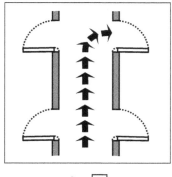 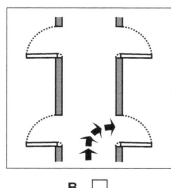 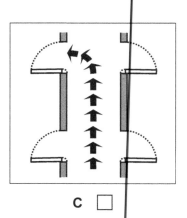

A ☐   B ☐   C ☐

3. Which boy is Tom?

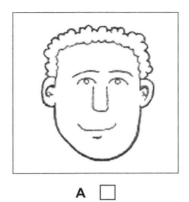 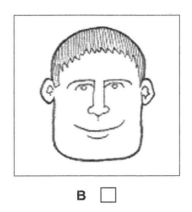 

A ☐   B ☐   C ☐

4. Where is the letter?

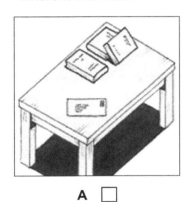 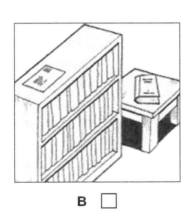 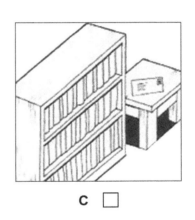

A ☐   B ☐   C ☐

5. What time does the film start?

 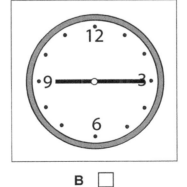 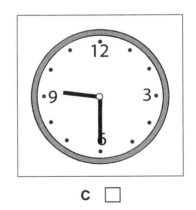

A ☐   B ☐   C ☐

6. Where is the speaker?

A ☐

B ☐

C ☐

7. Which is the correct picture?

A ☐

B ☐

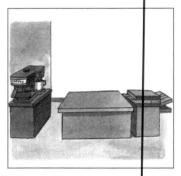

C ☐

8. Where is the speaker?

A ☐

B ☐

C ☐

9. Which student is ready to take the test?

A ☐

B ☐

C ☐

10. Which is the correct picture?

A ☐

B ☐

C ☐

Tip strip
6: Who is speaking? What is due today?

8: Where is the event? Who can go?

9: What can they have on the desk? Where should they put books?

Section 2

11. You will hear a recording about friends. Listen to the whole recording once. Then you will hear the recording again with pauses for you to write down what you hear. Make sure you spell the words correctly.

Tip strip
- Listen carefully and try to use your knowledge of grammar to get the endings right.
- If you miss a word, don't worry. Try to keep up. You can go back and guess the missing word from the context before you move on to the next section.
- Remember to check for spelling and grammar when you have finished the task.

Section 3

12–16 You will hear a recorded message. First, read the notes below, then listen and complete the notes with information from the recorded message. You will hear the recording twice.

> **Example:** Message for: *Paul*

12. Day of party: ....

13. Date of party: ....

14. Time of party: ....

15. Address: ....

16. Phone number: ....

17–21 You will hear a phone message. First, read the notes below, then listen and complete the notes with information from the phone message. You will hear the recording twice.

> **Example:** Message from: *June*

17. Family name: ....

18. Country to visit: ....

19. Number of people: ....

20. Length of holiday: ....

21. Phone number: ....

Tip strip

13: Listen for the <u>date</u> of the party.
14: Listen for information about the time of the party. When do they need to arrive?

16: You are listening for a phone number – write all the numbers you hear.
17: The speaker spells out the family name – write the letters you hear.

18: Where do they want to go on holiday?
20: Listen for information about the holiday. How long do they want to go away for?

Section 4

Read each text and put a cross (✗) by the missing word or phrase, as in the example.

Example:

> For payment, we .... cash and credit cards only –
> no cheques please.

A ☐ give

B ☒ accept

C ☐ show

22.

> For ....
> ## *Ford Fiesta*
> *40,000* kilometres
> Colour: *Silver*
> Year: *2008*
> *Good condition   Good price*
> **Phone 07793 415640**

A ☐ sale

B ☐ show

C ☐ example

23.

> **Please keep your .... off the seats on this train.**

A ☐ arms

B ☐ tickets

C ☐ feet

24.

Can you get your homework _____ your bags
and give it to me, please.

A ☐ into

B ☐ near

C ☐ out of

25.

Please _____ this message to Mr Jones. He is
teaching in his classroom 6E at the moment.

A ☐ carry

B ☐ take

C ☐ move

26.

Dear parents, we have a class _____ next
Wednesday. We're going to the museum.
Your child needs to bring a drink and a snack.

A ☐ teacher

B ☐ visit

C ☐ lesson

Tip strip

22: Think about the information – what is it for?

24: Think about where the homework is. Which option is suitable?

25: Which verb goes with "this message to …"?

Section 5

For each question, put a cross (✗) in the box below the correct picture, as in the example.

Example:

This is a photo of my cousin, Dan. He is with Rex, the family dog. Dan is only six, but he's really clever.

Which picture shows Dan?

A ☐   B ✗   C ☐

27.

In the evenings, I usually read a book or watch TV, but tonight I am going to do my homework on my computer.

What will Tom do tonight?

A ☐   B ☐   C ☐

28.

> ### LOST
> # Schoolbag
> **It has a pattern of five flowers inside a big heart.**
> *If you find it, please take it to the school office.*

Which is the correct picture?

A ☐

B ☐

C ☐

29.

> The school is just past the sports centre. It's the building on the left, opposite the shopping centre in Andrews Street.

Which is the correct map?

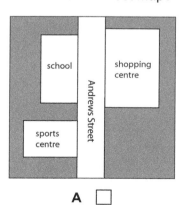

A ☐

B ☐

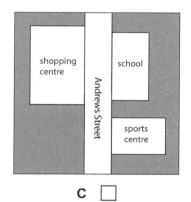

C ☐

Tip strip

27: The word "but" tells you he is going to do something different from what he "usually" does.
28: How many flowers are on the bag? Where are they?

30.

> Sorry, Amy,
> I can't see you for lunch today, I can't go out.
> I only have time to get a sandwich from the machine.
> John

What is John having for lunch?

A ☐

B ☐

C ☐

31.

> Hi, Mike,
> We're busy at the house just now. I finished painting the sitting room yesterday. We've got a lot to do today. Lucy is going to plant some fruit trees in the garden and I'm going to tidy the garage. Hope you're enjoying your holiday.
> Mark

What job will Mark do next?

A ☐

B ☐

C ☐

Tip strip

30: What <u>doesn't</u> he have time to do today? So, what will he have for lunch?

31: What job has Mark finished? Who is going to work in the garden?

Section 6

Read the notice below and answer the questions.

> Mrs Brown is running the art club again for the next ten weeks. This term the club is not on Tuesdays, but on Thursdays. It is at lunchtime from 12.30 to 1.30. Lessons start again at 1.45p.m. Please note that for the first week the art room is not free, so the class is in the hall.

Example: Who runs the art club? _Mrs Brown_

32. How many weeks does the club last? ....

33. What day of the week is the art club this term? ....

34. What time does the art club finish? ....

35. Where is the first class? ....

Read the email below and answer the questions.

> Hi, Bushra, I'm on holiday in Dubai. The people and the shopping here are great, but the view from my room in the Gate Hotel isn't very good. The weather is very hot, too. Next week I'm going to Cairo, then Athens and Rome. See you in a month, Cathy

Example: Who is the email from? _Cathy_

36. Who is Cathy writing to? ....

37. What things does Cathy like about her holiday? ....

38. What's wrong with Cathy's room? ....

39. Where is Cathy going first after Dubai? ....

Tip strip

32: How long is the art club running for?

33: Look for something different this term.
35: Is the art room free in the first week?

37: Be careful. Cathy talks about two things she likes about her holiday. What are they?
38: This is something Cathy didn't like.

Section 7

Read the email and complete the notes. Write **no more than three words** in each gap from the email.

Tip strip
- Focus on the key words in the questions: they will tell you exactly what information you need to find in the text.
- Sometimes it is easier to complete the notes when you change them to questions.

40: Which day are they meeting?

41: Where is the train going? Where does Duane need to take the bus from?

43: You are looking for a place where Marcel will be.

46: Can Duane ring Marcel? What does Marcel ask him to do?

Hi, Duane,

I can't meet you on Tuesday, but is Wednesday OK? To get to Fronton, take the train to Hornville. Then take a number 27 or 47 bus. The 27 is faster and cheaper. There's a Custa Café opposite the bus station. I will see you there. You can sleep in my bedroom, and I'll sleep in the lounge. I haven't got any bread for breakfast, so it'll be ham and eggs.

Let me know what time you will arrive. Don't ring me at work. Send an email.

Marcel

Example: Email to: *Duane*

---

40. Meet Marcel on: ....

41. Bus leaves from: ....

42. Best bus is: ....

43. Meet Marcel at: ....

44. Marcel to sleep in: ....

45. Breakfast is: ....

46. Contact Marcel by: ....

Use the information in **Section 7** to help you write your answer.

Tip strip

- Choose information from the Section 7 text that relates to what you are asked to do, but use your own language and <u>do not copy</u> large parts from the text.
- Make sure that you include all the points from the exam task and that you have written between 30 and 50 words.
- When you have finished, remember to check your grammar and spelling.

47. You have read the email to Duane. Now write Duane's reply to Marcel.
Write 30 to 50 words and include the following information:

- thank Marcel for his email
- say what time you will meet him
- tell him what you will bring
- ask him about the weather

Use your own words.

Tip strip

- Before you choose an option, think about the vocabulary you will need to use in your writing.
- Make a short, rough plan of the ideas you want to include and note down any key words.
- Don't forget to check your grammar and spelling when you have finished writing, and that you have written between 50 and 80 words.

48. Choose **one** of the topics below and write your answer in **50–80 words**.

    A   Write a short story about the picture.

    B   Describe the picture.

Section 10 (1.5 minutes)

In this section you will speak on your own for about a minute. Listen to what your teacher/examiner asks. Your teacher/examiner will ask one of the main questions below, and the follow-up questions if necessary.

Tip strip
- Remember it is quite natural to pause very briefly for thought when you are speaking.
- When the examiner asks you follow-up questions, try to avoid one-word answers.

Preliminary prompt 1:	*Do you live in a town or village?*
Main prompt 1:	*Tell me about your town/village.*
Follow-up prompts:	• *How big is your town/village?*
	• *What shops are there in your town/village?*
	• *Where do you go in your free time?*
	• *Do you have many friends there?*

Preliminary prompt 2:	*Do you live in a house or an apartment?*
Main prompt 2:	*Tell me about your house/apartment.*
Follow-up prompts:	• *What rooms has it got?*
	• *Where do you eat your meals?*
	• *How many people live in your house/apartment?*
	• *Do you like your house/apartment? Why/Why not?*

Preliminary prompt 3:	*What is the name of your school/college? (For test takers at school)*
Main prompt 3:	*Tell me about your school/college.*
Follow-up prompts:	• *How do you travel to school/college?*
	• *What time do you start/finish school/college?*
	• *What is your favourite subject?*
	• *Do you like your school/college? Why/Why not?*

Preliminary prompt 4:	*Who do you work for?*
Main prompt 4:	*Tell me about your job. (For test takers at work)*
Follow-up prompts:	• *What days do you work?*
	• *What time do you start/finish work?*
	• *How do you travel to your job?*
	• *Do you like your job? Why/Why not?*

There is no **Section 11** in PTE General Level A1.

Section 12 (2 minutes)

In this section you will talk about this picture for up to 1 minute. Your teacher/examiner will say:

Please tell me what you can see and what is happening in the picture.

Tell your teacher/examiner what you can see and what is happening in the picture.

Your teacher/examiner may ask you some of the following questions if necessary.

- *Where are they?*
- *What is the girl's present?*
- *What is the man/woman/little sister doing?*
- *What are the girls wearing?*
- *What can you see outside?*

Tip strip

- If you find you can't remember (or don't know) the right word for something, don't worry – try to get round the problem by saying something like: *I can't remember what it's called but it's one of those things for ...-ing.*

Section 13 (1.5 minutes)

In this section you will take part in a role play. Your teacher/examiner will explain the situation.

Your teacher/examiner is the shop assistant. Below is a sample script that your teacher/examiner may use.

We are in the supermarket. I am a shop assistant and you are a customer looking for something.

Ready? I'll start.

- *Hello/Good morning/Good afternoon. Can I help you?*
- *Yes, here is the (lemonade, depending on what the student asks for)*
- *They are on the left.*
- *It costs / They cost £2.00*
- *Would you like anything else?*

Thank you. That is the end of the test.

Tip strip
- What would you say in real life in this situation? Take time to understand the situation and just be as natural as possible.

Practice Test 2

Section 1

You will have 10 seconds to read each question. Listen and put a cross (✗) in the box next to the correct answer, as in the example. You have 10 seconds to choose the correct option.

Example: Which table does the woman want?

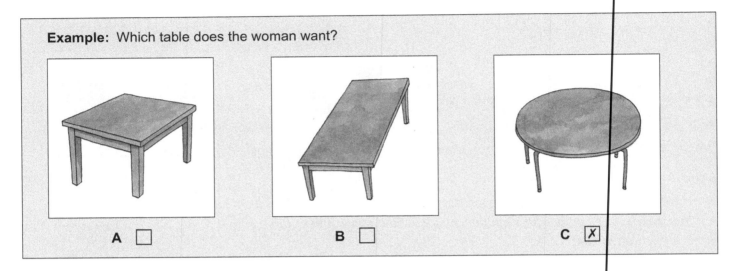

A ☐   B ☐   C ☒

1. What's the weather like now?

A ☐   B ☐   C ☐

2. What was Julie wearing yesterday?

A ☐   B ☐   C ☐

3. Where are the cups now?

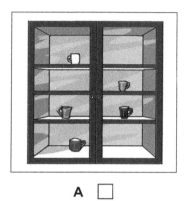

A ☐

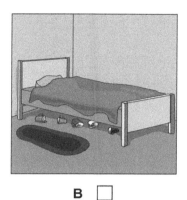

B ☐

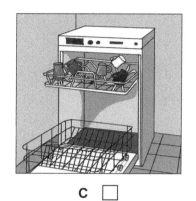

C ☐

4. Where is the boy going next week?

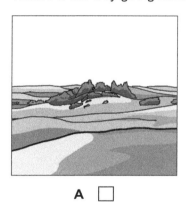

A ☐

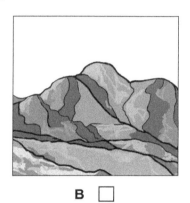

B ☐

C ☐

5. Which cottage is the man describing?

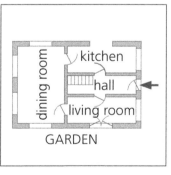

A ☐

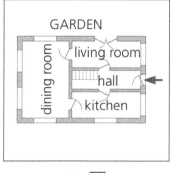

B ☐

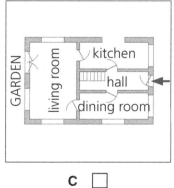

C ☐

6. What's Emma's problem?

A ☐

B ☐

C ☐

7. What does the speaker have a problem with?

A ☐

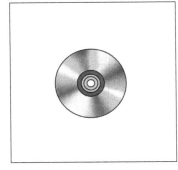

B ☐

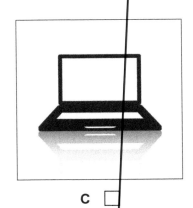

C ☐

8. Where are they?

A ☐

B ☐

C ☐

9. What does John have to wear?

A ☐

B ☐

C ☐

10. Which is his grandfather's house?

A ☐

B ☐

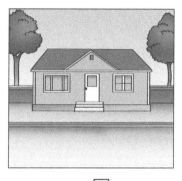

C ☐

Section 2

11. You will hear a recording about Ann's friend. Listen to the whole recording once. Then you will hear the recording again with pauses for you to write down what you hear. Make sure you spell the words correctly.

Section 3

12–16 You will hear a presentation on healthy living. First, read the notes below, then listen and complete the notes with information from the presentation. You will hear the recording twice.

> **Example:** This information is sometimes given by _doctors_

12. Start the morning with: ....

13. Examples of good snacks: ....

14. How to use stairs: ....

15. Bad for your health: ....

16. Amount of sleep our body needs: ....

17–21 You will hear a phone message. First, read the notes below, then listen and complete the notes with information from the message. You will hear the recording twice.

> **Example:** Message from: _Judith_

17. Message about: ....

18. She's made .... sandwiches.

19. She is also taking some ....

20. She has a packet of .... for everyone.

21. Fruit that she is taking: ....

Read each text and put a cross (✗) by the missing word or phrase, as in the example.

Example:

> ## *Mountain Walking Club*
> *Do you like walking in the mountains?*
> *Are you looking for new friends?*
> .... **the walking club for free!**
> This month only!

A ☐ Be

B ✗ Join

C ☐ Go

22.

> **Important:**
> Will all parents and other .... please report to reception (first door on the left, opposite the head teacher's office).
> Thank you

A ☐ doctors

B ☐ visitors

C ☐ bus drivers

23.

> ← → 🔍
>
> **Opening times:** 9.00–18.00 Tuesday–Sunday
> **Closed:** Mondays
> **Admission:** ....
>
> School groups of more than 15 and students should book in advance.

A ☐ Free

B ☐ Charge

C ☐ Price

24.

> ## *Welcome!*
> Please .... to be served.
> Ask about our cake of the day!

A ☐ eat

B ☐ see

C ☐ wait

25.

> ## The Old Picture House
> ### *Special Offer!*
> Two .... for the price of one!
> Friday night only
> Book online now to avoid disappointment.

A ☐ desks

B ☐ drinks

C ☐ tickets

26.

> ## Boots for young and old
> *Great prices!*
> All .... !
> Ideal for walking in the mountains!
> *Best quality!*

A ☐ figures

B ☐ sizes

C ☐ pairs

Section 5

For each question, put a cross (✗) in the box below the correct picture, as in the example.

Example:

This is a photo of my cousin, Dan. He is with Rex, the family dog. Dan is only six, but he's really clever.

Which picture shows Dan?

A ☐

B ☒

C ☐

27.

I know that park; I go skateboarding there most weekends. Not yesterday, though. We went to see my grandparents. It was my grandma's birthday.

What did he do yesterday?

A ☐

B ☐

C ☐

28.

> I miss our old place. It looked out over the park. All I can see now is the main road. And there's no garden either.

What can she see from her window now?

A ☐

B ☐

C ☐

29.

> ***Different ways of getting here:***
> *The fastest is flying.*
> *Trains, but they can be very expensive.*
> *Ferry costs the least, but it's very slow.*
> *Jane*

What is the cheapest way to get there?

A ☐

B ☐

C ☐

30.

> The new shopping centre is always crowded, but it is a good place to buy smart dresses and suits. The worst thing is its car park.

What can you buy at the centre?

A ☐

B ☐

C ☐

31.

> In the morning, we always play football in the park. Then we sit by the lake and have our sandwiches. After that, we go home.

Where do they go in the morning?

A ☐

B ☐

C ☐

Section 6

Read the notice below and answer the questions.

THE EDEN HOTEL is next to a beautiful sandy beach. We offer three meals a day and evening activities. Parents can relax in the restaurant because there is a special "fun room" where trained assistants look after the children. The rooms are large and we can add an extra bed if you need it. Stay at our luxurious hotel!

Example: Where is the hotel? _Next to a beach_

32 How many meals can you have each day? ....

33. What can parents do? ....

34. What do the trained assistants do? ....

35. What size are the rooms? ....

Read the information below and answer the questions.

Trent Summer School is a one-week intensive course for anyone who wishes to learn painting.

Students learn a wide range of techniques.
Our workshops are held in our art gallery.
Accommodation is included in the program,
but for food you need to pay £50.
There are no classes in the evenings,
but you can use the library if you wish.

Example: What is the name of the summer school? _Trent Summer School_

36. How long is the course? ....

37. Where are the workshops? ....

38. How much is the food? ....

39. What can you do in the evening? ....

Read the advertisement and complete the notes. Write **no more than three words** in each gap from the advertisement.

TOTON SWIMMING POOL
Opens on Friday, 1st June.

Prices are £5.00 for adults and £2.00 for people over sixty.
Children under twelve can swim for free, but only with an adult.
Adults must use our learner pool to teach children to swim.
The pool will be open from Monday to Saturday from 8 a.m. to 6 p.m.
All swimmers must wear a swim cap and a swimming costume. No shorts.
Group swimming lessons are available during term-time.
For more information about registration, please send an email.

Example: Advertisement for: *Toton swimming pool*

40. Opening date: ....

41. Price for children: ....

42. Children can practise swimming in: ....

43. On Tuesday, the pool closes at: ....

44. Don't wear: ....

45. You can have group lessons: ....

46. For more information: ....

Section 8

Use the information in **Section 7** to help you write your answer.

47. You have read the text about Toton swimming pool. Now write an email to your friend and ask her/him to go to the swimming pool with you. **Write 30–50 words** and include the following information:

- tell her/him about the new swimming pool
- say when you want to go
- suggest where to meet
- suggest how to go there

Use your own words.

Section 9

48. Choose **one** of the topics below and write your answer in **50–80 words**.

A   Write a short story about the picture.

B   Describe the picture.

Section 10 (1.5 minutes)

In this section you will speak on your own for about a minute. Listen to what your teacher/examiner asks. Your teacher/examiner will ask one of the main questions below, and the follow-up questions if necessary.

Preliminary prompt 1:   *Do you use a computer?*

Main prompt 1:   *Tell me what you use your computer for.*

Follow-up prompts:
- *How many hours do you use a computer every day?*
- *Do you do your homework on a computer?*
- *How did you learn to use a computer?*
- *Do you use email? Why/Why not?*

Preliminary prompt 2:   *Do you like travelling in your country?*

Main prompt 2:   *Tell me about a beautiful place to visit in your country.*

Follow-up prompts:
- *Do you like travelling by car or train?*
- *How often do you travel?*
- *Who do you usually go with?*
- *Do you like to travel with your friends? Why/Why not?*

Preliminary prompt 3:   *Do you like your town/city?*

Main prompt 3:   *Tell me about where you live.*

Follow-up prompts:
- *How often do you meet your neighbours?*
- *Are there a lot of shops in your area?*
- *How far are you from the city centre?*
- *Is there a lot of traffic in your area?*

Preliminary prompt 4:   *Do you use your mobile a lot?*

Main prompt 4:   *Tell me about what you use your mobile for.*

Follow-up prompts:
- *When do you switch off your mobile?*
- *How many hours a day do you use your mobile?*
- *Do you spend much money on your mobile?*
- *Do you listen to music on your mobile?*

There is no **Section 11** in PTE General Level A1.

Section 12 (2 minutes)

In this section you will talk about a picture for up to 1 minute. Your teacher/examiner will say:

Please tell me what you can see and what is happening in the picture.

Tell your teacher/examiner what you can see and what is happening in the picture.

Your teacher/examiner may ask you some of the following questions if necessary.

- *What are they doing?*
- *How old are the children?*
- *What is the boy doing?*
- *What can you see on the table?*
- *Describe the cake.*

In this section you will take part in a role play. Your teacher/examiner will explain the situation.

Test taker's card

You are in a coffee shop and want to order a drink.
The examiner works in the coffee shop.

- Say what you want to drink.
- Decide what to eat and ask for it.
- Ask how much it is.
- Ask if you can pay by card.

Your teacher/examiner works in the coffee shop. Below is a sample script that your teacher/examiner may use.

We are in a coffee shop. I work in the coffee shop and you want to order a drink.

Ready? I'll start.

- *Good afternoon, can I help you?*
- *Certainly. Would you like something to eat as well?*
- *Here you are.*
- *It's £6.00.*
- *Of course. You can pay in cash or by card.*

Thank you. That is the end of the test.

Exam Guide

Section 1: Graphical multiple choice

What is being tested?
Section 1 tests your ability to understand the main idea of a short spoken text.

What do you have to do?
Answer ten questions. For each question, you will listen to a short recording with one speaker. You will hear each recording once. For each one, you will see a question and three possible picture options (A, B and C). You have to listen to the recording and the question and decide which picture answers the question best.

Strategy

- Read and listen to the instructions.
- For each question, you will have 10 seconds to read the question and check the picture options. Pictures can sometimes look very similar; think about what is different in each picture.
- Remember that you have only one chance to listen.
- Put a cross in the box next to the picture you think answers the question best.

- The questions are marked as either correct or incorrect. If you are not sure, choose the picture you think is most likely – you may be right.

Preparation tips

- Try to get used to hearing a range of voices and accents. Search online for an English language radio programme on a topic that interests you. You won't understand every word, but listen and try to get the key ideas as you listen.

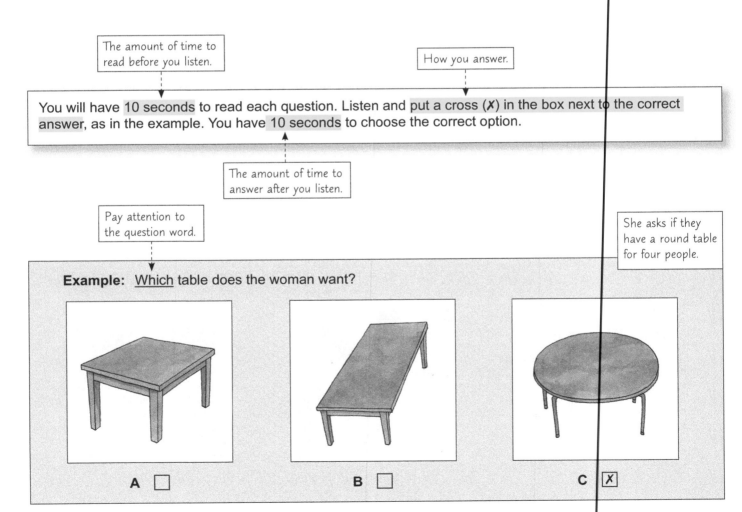

The amount of time to read before you listen.

How you answer.

You will have **10 seconds** to read each question. Listen and **put a cross (✗) in the box next to the correct answer**, as in the example. You have **10 seconds** to choose the correct option.

The amount of time to answer after you listen.

Pay attention to the question word.

She asks if they have a round table for four people.

Example: <u>Which</u> table does the woman want?

A ☐   B ☐   C ☒

Section 2: Dictation

What is being tested?

Section 2 assesses listening and writing skills. It tests your ability to understand an extended piece of speech by transcribing a spoken text.

What do you have to do?

Listen to one person speaking and write exactly what you hear with correct spellings. You will hear the recording twice; the second time with pauses, giving you time to write down word-for-word what you hear. There is one dictation to complete and therefore only one recording.

Strategy

- Read and listen to the instructions.
- Pay attention to the topic of the recording.
- During the first reading of the dictation, listen very carefully to the whole recording. The topic is always given in the instructions. Try to understand the overall extract and pick out some key words. If you write the key words as you hear them, you will have a better chance of recognising the topic vocabulary and words that go together.
- You will hear the recording for a second time. This time with pauses giving you time to write the words down. If you miss or misunderstand a word during the second listening, leave a space and keep writing.
- When the dictation has finished, read it through and use your knowledge of the topic vocabulary and grammar to help you guess any missing words. If what you have written down doesn't

make sense, then you have probably misheard it, so consider changing it to something that sounds similar and makes sense.

- Check you have spelt the words correctly.

Preparation tips

- Improve your general listening skills: practise listening to a topic and understanding the main ideas. Search online for an English language radio programme on a topic that interests you or for public announcements:
  - You won't understand every word, but listen and try to note down the key words as you listen.
  - Practise picking out the key words; these are usually words that the speaker stresses.
  - Practise listening and writing the key words down at the same time.
  - Use your knowledge of grammar to get word endings right.

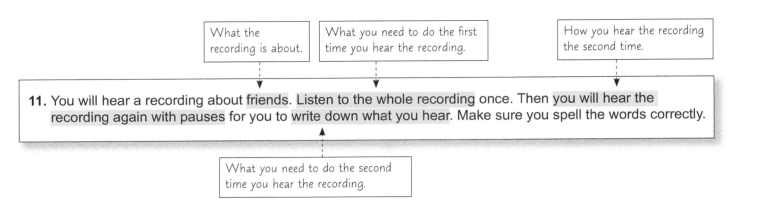

What the recording is about.

What you need to do the first time you hear the recording.

How you hear the recording the second time.

11. You will hear a recording about friends. Listen to the whole recording once. Then you will hear the recording again with pauses for you to write down what you hear. Make sure you spell the words correctly.

What you need to do the second time you hear the recording.

Section 3: Text, note completion

What is being tested?

Section 3 tests your ability to extract specific information from extended spoken texts.

What do you have to do?

Listen to two recordings (monologues) and complete notes or sentences for each using the information you have heard. There are ten gaps to complete; five per task. You will hear each recording twice.

Strategy

- Read and listen to the instructions.
- You will hear two recordings. For each recording, you will have five questions to answer. For each recording, you will have 30 seconds to prepare. Read the notes carefully and see what kind of information is missing, then listen to the recording.
- Try to make notes while you listen to the recording.
- Listen to the recording for a second time. Then read the notes again and try to complete them.

Preparation tips

- Improve your general listening skills. Search online for an English language programme or a recording on a topic that interests you. There are a lot of websites that provide practise materials for different levels. You won't understand every word, but listen and try to note down the key words as you listen.

This is what the recording is.

What you need to do before you listen.

How you answer.

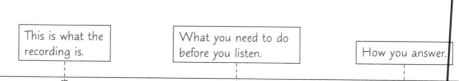

12–16 You will hear a recorded message. First, read the notes below, then listen and complete the notes with information from the recorded message. You will hear the recording twice.

Check your notes the second time you hear the recording and complete any gaps.

Example: Message <u>for</u>: *Paul*

Underline the key words.

Section 4: Gap fill 3-option multiple-choice

What is being tested?

Section 4 tests your ability to understand the main idea of short written texts.

What do you have to do?

Answer five questions. Read five short texts, each containing a gap, and choose which of three answer options is the missing word or phrase. There are five gaps to complete; one per text.

- Read the instructions carefully.
- Read each question and the three options carefully and highlight or underline any key words. Think about what is different in each option.
- When you have chosen your answer, check the other options again to make sure they cannot be correct.
- Re-read the text with your selected option to check that the text makes sense (in terms of meaning). If it doesn't, you will need to review your answer.

- Do as many practice tests as possible so that you fully understand the task and what you should do.
- Ask yourself what type of text it is and why it was written.
- Practise highlighting or underlining the key words in the text and using this information to consider the meaning of the missing words. You can practise this by working with a partner: choose one text each, remove some words from the text, and then swap them. Underline the key words and try to understand what information is missing.
- Keep a vocabulary notebook in which you write down useful vocabulary you come across, arranged by topic.
- When you learn a new word, write down not only the word, but also the sentence it is used in.

How you answer.

Read each text and put a cross (✗) by the missing word or phrase, as in the example.

Underline the key words.

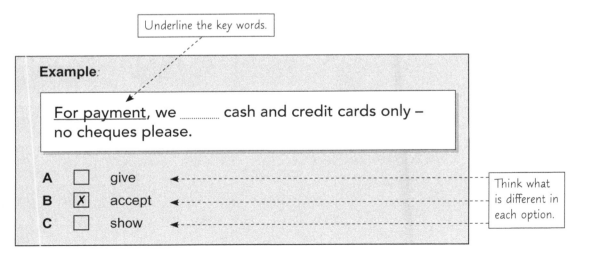

Example:

<u>For payment</u>, we _____ cash and credit cards only – no cheques please.

A ☐ give

B ☒ accept

C ☐ show

Think what is different in each option.

Section 5: 3-option graphical multiple choice

What is being tested?

Section 5 tests your ability to understand the main idea of a short written text.

What do you have to do?

Read five short texts. There is a question for each text and three picture options. Choose the picture that answers the question best.

Strategy

- Before you read each text, look at the pictures carefully so you are clear what each one shows and how they are different.
- Read the text and the question and underline the key words.
- Then look at the pictures and choose the one that answers the question best.
- Check the other options to make sure they don't match.

Preparation tips

- Do as many practice tests as possible so that you fully understand the task and what you should do.
- Read as much as you can in your free time. The reading that you do outside the classroom will help you become a better reader.

How you answer.

For each question, put a cross (✗) in the box below the correct picture, as in the example.

Underline the key words and information in the text.

The photo is of a boy, Dan, and a dog, so the correct answer is B.

Example:

This is <u>a photo of my cousin</u>, Dan. <u>He</u> is with <u>Rex, the family dog</u>. Dan is only six, but he's really clever.

<u>Which picture</u> shows <u>Dan</u>?

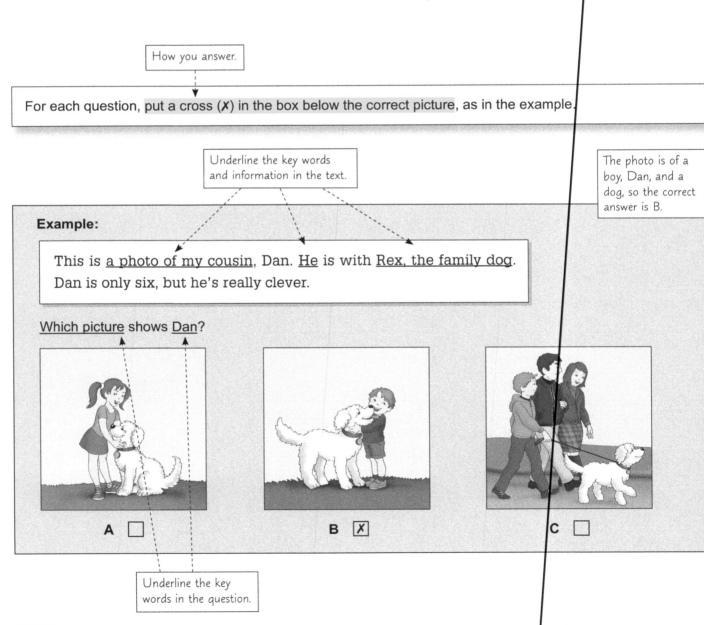

A ☐   B ✗   C ☐

Underline the key words in the question.

Section 6: Open-ended question

What is being tested?

Section 6 tests your ability to understand the main points of short written texts.

What do you have to do?

Read two texts and answer eight questions about them using single words or short answers. There are eight questions to answer; four per text.

- Before you read the text, read the questions and focus on the key words. These are often questions words such as *what*, *why*, *how*, *when*.
- Pay attention to the key words, they will tell you exactly what information you need to find.
- Try to answer each question briefly and accurately using words from the text where appropriate.
- Try to avoid writing long answers with unnecessary information. Your answer doesn't have to be written as a sentence – often a word or phrase is enough.
- To help you focus your thoughts, underline or highlight the area in the text where you think the answer is.

- Do as many practice tests as possible so that you fully understand the task and what you should do.
- Remember that Pearson Test of English General aims to test real-life skills. The reading that you do outside the classroom will help you become a better reader.
- Practise reading texts quickly all the way through to understand the main ideas. You could read notices in newspapers, magazines or online and summarise the main ideas in them, even if you don't know all the vocabulary.

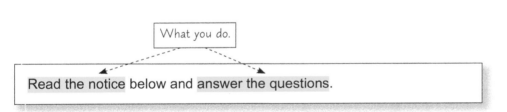

What you do.

Read the notice below and answer the questions.

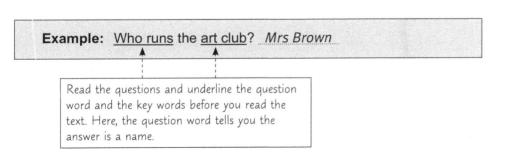

Example: Who runs the art club? *Mrs Brown*

Read the questions and underline the question word and the key words before you read the text. Here, the question word tells you the answer is a name.

Section 7: Text, note completion

What is being tested?

Section 7 tests your ability to extract specific information from an extended written text.

What do you have to do?

Read a text and use information from it to fill gaps in seven incomplete sentences or notes. You must use no more than three words from the text to do this. There are seven sentences or notes to complete and one source text.

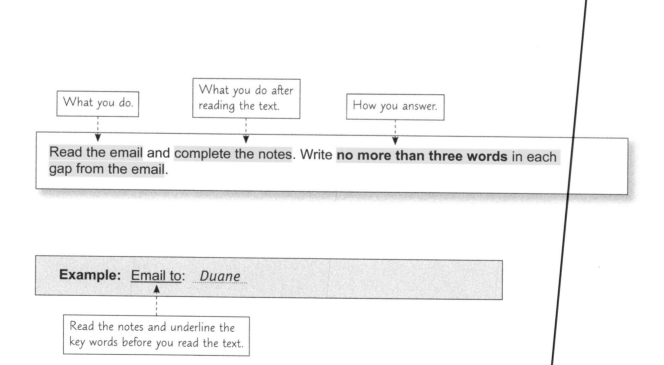

What you do.

What you do after reading the text.

How you answer.

Read the email and complete the notes. Write **no more than three words** in each gap from the email.

Example: Email to: *Duane*

Read the notes and underline the key words before you read the text.

Section 8: Write correspondence

What is being tested?

Section 8 tests your ability to write a piece of correspondence.

What do you have to do?

Write an email, a formal or informal letter, a postcard or a note based on information given in Section 7. There is one text to write (30–50 words). There is a "tolerated" word limit of 24–55 words for Section 8. If the response is below or over this limit, you will automatically score 0 for the section.

Strategy

- Read the instructions very carefully.

- Check task instructions to find out what you are writing and who you are writing to. You need to understand the purpose of the correspondence.

- Cover all the bullet points in your writing. Avoid writing too much about one and not enough about the others.

- Highlight or underline the parts of the text in Section 7 that you could use to plan the content of your answer. You will need to refer to the text in Section 7, usually by summarising the main idea and/or commenting on it. In either case, you should use your own words as far as possible. The *Writing Guide* on pages 54–58 provides some help with this.

- Leave a few minutes at the end of the task to check through your work.

- Check your writing for the accuracy of your grammar and spelling, and that you have written between 30 and 50 words.

Preparation tips

- Work on improving your vocabulary by reading and noting down words and expressions you might use to write on topics such as family, hobbies, work, travelling and shopping.

- Learn how to plan your writing and what information you need to include. Practise using linking words. Use the *Writing Guide* on pages 54–58, which also gives you useful language you can use.

- Understand what kind of mistakes you make in your writing and try to improve those areas. Build a list of your errors (for example, using a piece of past work marked by your teacher) as a guide.

- Practise checking through your work for spelling errors. Work with a partner to discuss content and organisation and to correct each other's language errors.

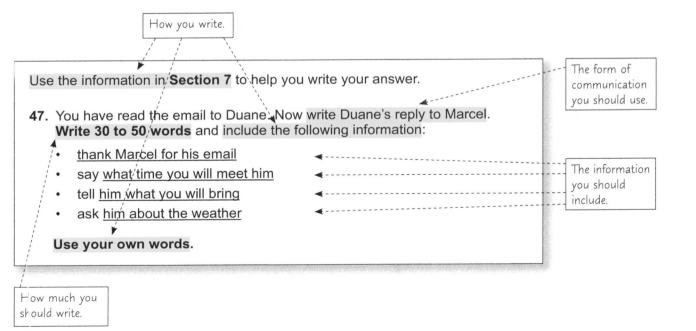

How you write.

Use the information in **Section 7** to help you write your answer.

47. You have read the email to Duane. Now write Duane's reply to Marcel. **Write 30 to 50 words** and include the following information:

- thank Marcel for his email
- say what time you will meet him
- tell him what you will bring
- ask him about the weather

Use your own words.

The form of communication you should use.

The information you should include.

How much you should write.

Section 9: Write text

What is being tested?

Section 9 tests your ability to write a short text based on a picture.

What do you have to do?

Write a piece of writing from a choice of two options. Choose one of two pictures. The form of the response may be a short story, a description or a diary entry. There is one text to write (50–80 words). There is a "tolerated" word limit of 30–88 words for Section 9. If the response is below or over this limit, you will automatically score 0 for the section.

Strategy

- Read the introduction to the task and choose one picture to write about.
- Think quickly about the vocabulary you need to use to make sure you know enough words to write your answer.
- Think what type of writing you need to produce (a story, a description or a diary entry) and what tense(s) you need to use.
- Try to use linking words to link your sentences.
- Leave a few minutes at the end of the task to check through your work.

- Check that your grammar and spelling is correct and that you have written 50 to 80 words.

Preparation tips

- Look at the *Writing Guide* on pages 54–58 for sample answers and useful language you can use in your writing.
- Work with a partner. Find a picture from a book or magazine and write a story or a description. Work with your partner to discuss content and to correct each other's language errors.

What you should do.

How much you should write.

48. Choose **one** of the topics below and write your answer in **50–80 words**.

A Write a short story about the picture.

B Describe the picture

Think about the topic and make a short plan of what you want to write.

Section 10: Sustained monologue

What is being tested?

Section 10 tests your ability to speak continuously about matters of personal information and interest.

What do you have to do?

Speak continuously about a familiar topic for up to 1 minute. The examiner might ask you some follow-up questions to encourage you to continue talking. The questions focus on regular and routine activities. This section of the test lasts 1.5 minutes.

Strategy

- You need to talk about a familiar topic on your own for about 1 minute.
- If you don't, the examiner may ask you some questions to encourage you to talk. Listen to the examiner's questions very carefully, before giving an answer. Try to give an answer which is more than just a few words.
- Remember that it is quite natural to pause very briefly for thought when you are speaking.

Preparation tips

- Make sure you are familiar with the task: what the examiner will do and how long the section is.
- Practise talking about yourself with other students, on a range of different topics. Choose a topic, for example, shopping, and ask each other different questions.
- Practise talking for about one minute on a topic, with a classmate timing you.
- Work on building your vocabulary on a range of familiar topics.
- Practise listening carefully to questions and thinking about the topic, before giving an answer.

How long you need to speak on your own.

In this section you will speak on your own for about a minute. Listen to what your teacher/examiner asks. Your teacher/examiner will ask one of the main questions below, and the follow-up questions if necessary.

Preliminary prompt 1:   *Do you live in a town or village?*

Main prompt 1:   *Tell me about your town/village.*

Follow-up prompts:
- *How big is your town/village?*
- *What shops are there in your town/village?*
- *Where do you go in your free time?*
- *Do you have many friends there?*

What the examiner will ask you.

Section 11: Discussion

There is no Section 11 in PTE General Level A1.

Section 12: Describe picture

What is being tested?

Section 12 tests your ability to speak continuously about a picture.

What do you have to do?

Speak without interruption about a picture that the examiner presents to you for up to 1 minute. Then answer any follow up questions that the examiner might ask you. This section of the test lasts 2 minutes.

Strategy

- The examiner will present you with a card and will ask you to describe a picture.
- Try to talk about the picture for about 1 minute.
- Describe the picture using sentences rather than single words.
- Look at the picture carefully; say what you see in the picture, who you think the people in the picture are, where they are, and what they are doing/wearing.
- The examiner may ask you some follow-up questions about the picture to encourage you to speak more.

Preparation tips

- Make sure you are familiar with the task: what you are expected to do, what materials you will be given, what the examiner will say and how long the task is.

- Practise describing a picture with other students. Ask each other different questions. Here is some useful language you can use:

  What is in the picture?

  This picture shows …

  There is / There are …

  I can see …

  What is happening?

  The man is …-ing

  The people are …-ing

  It's raining.

  Where in the picture?

  On the right / On the left …

  Under / Near / Behind / Next to / In front of …

  If something is not clear

  Maybe it's a …

  He might be a …

What you need to do.	How long you should speak for.

In this section you will talk about the picture for up to 1 minute. Your teacher/examiner will say:

Please tell me what you can see and what is happening in the picture.

Tell your teacher/examiner what you can see and what is happening in the picture.

> The instructions tell you that you can answer in the present tense; use both the present simple and present continuous tense.

Your teacher/examiner may ask you some of the following questions if necessary.

- *Where are they?*
- *What is the girl's present?*
- *What is the man/woman/little sister doing?*
- *What are the girls wearing?*
- *What can you see outside?*

> You might be asked some questions to help you speak for longer.

Section 13: Role play

What is being tested?

Section 13 tests your ability to perform and respond to language functions appropriately.

What do you need to do?

Take part in a role play with the examiner using a role card with information and instructions. This section of the test lasts 1.5 minutes.

Strategy

- The examiner will present you with a card.
- Listen to the examiner very carefully.
- You will be given 15 seconds to read the instructions and prepare.
- Try to think of some ideas based on the information on the card.
- If you are not sure what to do, ask the examiner.
- The examiner will say who should start the role play. For example, if the examiner is going to start, he/she will say: *Ready? I'll start.*
- You don't need acting skills to take part in the role play. Take time to understand the situation and just be as natural as possible.

Preparation tips

- Make sure you are familiar with the task: what you are expected to do, what the examiner will say, what materials you will be given, and how long the task is.
- Work with a partner. Practise different language functions, such as asking for directions/information, giving information, apologising and responding to an offer in different situations.
- Improve your vocabulary. Learn words that are related to different routine matters (for example, buying a ticket or making an appointment). This will help you to speak without too many pauses, when it is your time to talk.

What you will do.

In this section you will take part in a role play. Your teacher/examiner will explain the situation.

What your role is and what you are doing.

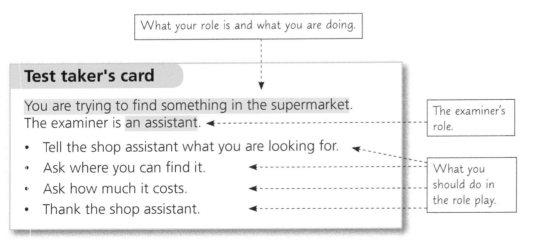

Test taker's card

You are trying to find something in the supermarket. The examiner is an assistant.

- Tell the shop assistant what you are looking for.
- Ask where you can find it.
- Ask how much it costs.
- Thank the shop assistant.

The examiner's role.

What you should do in the role play.

Writing Guide

Introduction

Writing tasks in Pearson Test of English General

In Pearson Test of English General, there are two sections which assess your writing skills.

Section 8

In Section 8, you are asked to write a piece of correspondence. This may take the form of an email, a letter, a postcard or a note.

What you have to write will always be a response to the text you read in Section 7. For example, you may be asked to write a postcard to a friend giving them information about the place you are visiting. You will need to refer to the text in the previous section. You should use your own words as far as possible, not simply copy parts of the original text. Exactly what you need to include is indicated by three or four bullet-pointed instructions.

The word limit in this section is **30–50 words**. You may well find that the biggest problem is not that this is a lot of words, but that, once you start writing, it is not enough to include everything that you want. For this reason, it is important to express yourself concisely.

Section 9

This section is a writing task in which you will need to write a short text based on a picture. What you are asked to write can take various forms. It may be a story, a description or a diary entry based on the picture.

There will be a choice of two tasks/pictures. The topics will be related to two of the themes of the test, so there may be ideas in other sections, but, again, you should use your own words. The word limit is **50–80 words**.

General advice

There are specific tips in the relevant test sections of this book and in the *Exam Guide*. Below are some more general pieces of advice relating to writing in general and in the Pearson Test of English General.

- Always be aware of the reader, the person or people that you are writing for. This will have an effect on both the content and the style of what you write. Generally speaking, an informal, more conversational style is best for letters and emails to friends.

- Don't pre-learn large sections and long phrases, for example, introductions, and try to fit them into your writing, whatever the topic. Firstly, it often looks unnatural and is usually easy for the examiner to notice. Secondly, it is often a waste of words: if you use a lot of words on "decoration", you might find you have no room left to say anything useful.

- Make a short plan of what you want to write. In this way, your writing will be clearer and better organised. Paragraphing makes the organisation of your writing clear. Linking words will also help to do this, but, if the writing is well organised, it does not need very many. It is probably enough to have two or three basic words or phrases for various purposes, for example, *and* or *also* for adding extra information and *but* for showing contrast. The most important thing is that you understand how to use them.

- When you have finished writing, check what you have written for mistakes, especially the ones you make under pressure and which you would get right if you thought about it. Try to be aware of the kinds of mistake you tend to make frequently.

- Your writing will be marked for how well it performs the task as well as for the language, so make sure you cover all the points required by the question and bullet points.

Postcard

Model answer

You have read about the plan for a school trip to London. Imagine you are on the trip. Now write a postcard to a friend. **Write 30–50 words** and include the following information:

- tell your friend where you are
- describe the city
- tell him/her what you are doing
- say why you like it

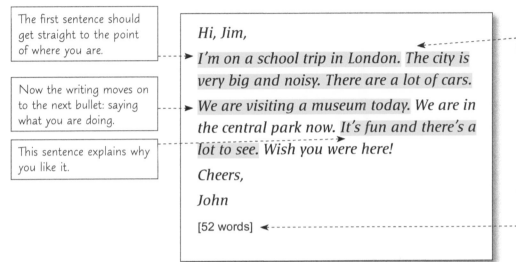

The first sentence should get straight to the point of where you are.

Now the writing moves on to the next bullet: saying what you are doing.

This sentence explains why you like it.

Hi, Jim,

I'm on a school trip in London. The city is very big and noisy. There are a lot of cars. We are visiting a museum today. We are in the central park now. It's fun and there's a lot to see. Wish you were here!

Cheers,

John

[52 words]

The next two sentences describe the city.

The word total of 52 words is slightly over the maximum number that the instructions ask you to write. If your answer is a few words longer or shorter, there won't be a penalty. Check the *Exam Guide* section for more information on the word count.

Describing things
It's nice/big/small.
There's a beautiful building …
There are some nice …

Describing feelings
I'm having a lovely/great time.
It is fun/exciting.
I like/enjoy …-ing …

Note: invitation

Model answer

It's your birthday and you are having a party. Now write a note to invite a friend. **Write 30–50 words** and include the following information:

- say when the party is
- tell your friend what time the party starts
- describe what you will do at the party
- give her/him your home address

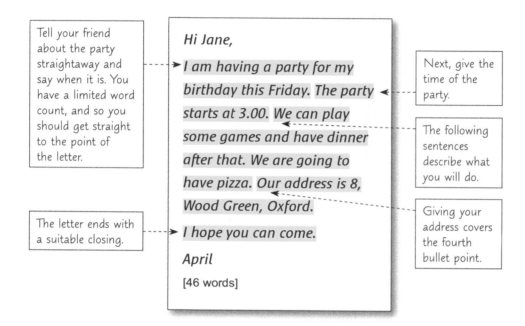

Tell your friend about the party straightaway and say when it is. You have a limited word count, and so you should get straight to the point of the letter.

The letter ends with a suitable closing.

Hi Jane,

I am having a party for my birthday this Friday. The party starts at 3.00. We can play some games and have dinner after that. We are going to have pizza. Our address is 8, Wood Green, Oxford.

I hope you can come.

April

[46 words]

Next, give the time of the party.

The following sentences describe what you will do.

Giving your address covers the fourth bullet point.

Useful language

Opening
Dear James,
Hi James,
It's always good to hear from you.
Thanks for your letter.
How are you?
I hope you're well.

Talking about time
It is on Thursday/Saturday.
It is at 5.00/5 o'clock/5 p.m./5 in the evening.
It is in the morning/afternoon/evening.

Closing
Yours
Best wishes
Write soon
See you
Thanks again
Hope to hear from you soon
Love

Email: invitation

Model answer

You have read an advert about a tour of the UK. Now write an email to a friend. **Write 30–50 words** and include the following information:

- tell your friend about the tour
- invite him/her to go with you
- say when the tour is
- suggest what you can do

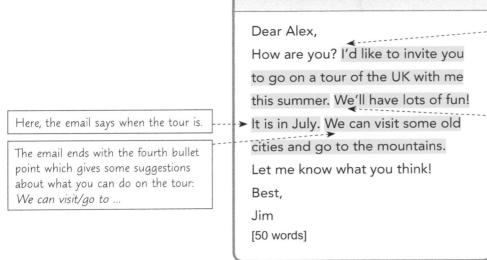

After a short, polite opening, the email gets straight to the first two bullet points: telling your friend about the tour and inviting him/her to go with you. You have a limited number of words, so it's important to get straight to the point and this sentence covers both bullet points together.

Here, the email says when the tour is.

The email ends with the fourth bullet point which gives some suggestions about what you can do on the tour: *We can visit/go to ...*

The email doesn't just give information, but also uses this expression to make the invitation sound interesting and fun for your friend.

Email content:

Dear Alex,

How are you? I'd like to invite you to go on a tour of the UK with me this summer. We'll have lots of fun! It is in July. We can visit some old cities and go to the mountains. Let me know what you think!

Best,

Jim

[50 words]

Useful language

Inviting
I want/would like to invite you to …
I hope you can come.
Would you like to …?

Explaining
I am happy because …
I like it because …
You'll enjoy it because …

Adding interest
We'll have fun!
It's really/very interesting!
There's a lot to do/see.

Email: apology

Model answer

You have received an invitation from Anna to her party, but you can't go. Now write an email to Anna. **Write 30–50 words** and include the following information:

- thank Anna for the invitation
- apologise for not going
- tell her why you can't go
- say when you can see her next

The email covers the first bullet point straightaway by thanking Anna for the invitation. You don't have many words in your word limit, so it is important to get straight to the point of the email.

but is used to link the two parts of the sentence.

Hi, Anna,

Thank you so much for inviting me to your party. I am really sorry, but I can't go. I have an exam next week, but we can meet after my exams.

We can go to the cinema.

Let me know

Love

Jenny

[44 words]

The second sentence makes the apology: *I am really sorry, but ...*

This sentence starts with the reason why you can't go and ends with a suggestion of when you can see her next, so it covers the last two bullet points.

Useful language

Thanking
I just wanted to thank you for …
Thank you so much for …

Apologising
I'm really sorry, but …
I'm so sorry that I can't …

Write a story

Model answer

Write a short story about the picture. Write your answer in **50–80 words**.

Start by describing the picture. Write about the people: who they are, where they are and what they are doing.

It is a nice and sunny day. I am with my family. We are waiting for the bus because we are going on holiday. We only have two big suitcases. I have a small bag. We are not going very far. We are going to the beach and we will stay there for two days. We can swim and play on the beach. I love swimming. We are all very excited.

[71 words]

Give reasons for things.

Write about some details in the picture.

Imagine what is happening.

Describe feelings. This makes a good ending for your short story.

Useful language

Describing people

My sister is … years old.
My father is wearing …
My mother is tall/short.
My sister has short/long/dark/blonde hair.

Writing about yourself

I'm good at …
I really like/don't like …-ing.
I enjoy/love …-ing.
I'm not good at …-ing.
I don't like/enjoy …-ing.
My favourite … is …

Writing about others

There are three people in my family.
My sister doesn't like …-ing.
My father enjoys …-ing.
My mother works in a …
My father doesn't drive.
They don't like …-ing.
We love …-ing.

Giving reasons

… because …

Describe picture

Model answer

Describe the picture. Write your answer in **50–80 words**.

Start by describing the people in the picture: what time it is, where they are and what they are doing.

It is eight o'clock in the morning. I am in the office. I work on the twentieth floor. My office is nice. It has very big windows. I sometimes look at the sky and have a cup of coffee.

I have a lot of work today. I am talking to people on the phone. I have a lot of things to read, too. It is a busy day today. I like it when I am very busy.

[77 words]

Find some details in the picture to describe.

Say what is happening in the picture.

Look at the people's faces and actions to help you describe their feelings.

Useful language

What is happening
She is ...-ing
We are ...-ing
I am drinking/eating/making ...

Describing things
a big office/house/city ...
a sunny/cold/warm day ...
... big windows ...
... old books ...
There is/are ... on the desk.
Some / Many / A few books are ...

Audioscript

Practice Test 1

Section 1

Narrator: You will have 10 seconds to read each question. Listen and put a cross (✗) in the box next to the correct answer, as in the example. You have 10 seconds to choose the correct option.

Example

Listen to the woman. Which table does she want?

Woman: Excuse me. I'm looking for a round table. A round table for four people. Do you have any?

Narrator: The correct answer is C.

Number 1

Listen to the man. Which hotel is he speaking about?

Man: Well, it's quite big. There are six floors and it's got a swimming pool. It's close to a river.

Narrator: **Number 2**

Listen to the woman. Which is the bathroom door?

Woman: Do you want the bathroom, Mike? It's the second door on the right.

Narrator: **Number 3**

Listen to the girl. Which boy is Tom?

Girl: My brother, Tom, is in your maths class at college. Do you know him? He's got short, curly hair.

Narrator: **Number 4**

Listen to the woman. Where is the letter?

Woman: Oh, Gina! The letter's on the little table next to the bookcase.

Narrator: **Number 5**

Listen to the girl. What time does the film start?

Girl: Dad! You don't need to hurry. The film starts at half past nine, not nine fifteen.

Narrator: **Number 6**

Listen to the speaker. Where is he?

Man: Please submit your homework to me by 5 p.m. Your homework is due today.

Narrator: **Number 7**

Listen to the speaker. Which is the correct picture?

Man: The photocopier is on the desk. It's near the coffee machine.

Narrator: **Number 8**

Listen to the speaker. Where is he?

Man: Your attention, please. The fifth-grade speech contest will start at 9 o'clock in the library. All teachers and students are welcome.

Narrator: **Number 9**

Listen to the teacher's instructions. Which student is ready to take the test?

Woman: Before you start the test, you should have two pencils on your desk. You should also place all books under your desk before you take the test.

Narrator: **Number 10**

Listen to the man. Which is the correct picture?

Man: For my birthday, I am not going to have a party in my house this year. I was thinking of dinner in a restaurant or bowling, and I chose dinner.

Section 2

Narrator: **Number 11**

You will hear a recording about friends. Listen to the whole recording once. Then you will hear the recording again with pauses for you to write down what you hear. Make sure you spell the words correctly.

Man: I have a lot of friends. We like sport. We play tennis and go swimming.

Narrator: Now listen again and write down your answer.

Man: I have a lot of friends. // We like sport. // We play tennis // and go swimming.

Section 3

Narrator: **Numbers 12–16**

You will hear a recorded message. First, read the notes below, then listen and complete the notes with information from the recorded message. You will hear the recording twice.

Woman: This is a message for Paul. How are you? I am having a party on Friday night. This Friday, the seventeenth of July, and I want you to come. Please arrive at 8 o'clock in the evening. My address is 11 Roseberry Road. That's Roseberry, spelt R-o-s-e-b-e-r-r-y. Please reply by telephone on eight eight eight four three two oh. That's eight eight eight four three two oh. Look forward to seeing you. Goodbye.

Narrator: Now listen again.

Numbers 17–21

You will hear a phone message. First, read the notes below, then listen and complete the notes with information from the phone message. You will hear the recording twice.

Woman: Hello. My name is June Waite. June like the month, and Waite, W-A-I-T-E. I'm phoning about holidays in China in September when it's not too hot. There are four adults in the group and no children. We want to go for two weeks, and visit different places. I'm going to be at home all day. Can you phone me this afternoon? My number is seven five oh double one four. Seven five oh double one four. Bye.

Narrator: Now listen again.

That is the end of the listening section of the test. Now go on to the other sections of the test.

Practice Test 2

Section 1

Narrator: You will have 10 seconds to read each question. Listen and put a cross (✗) in the box next to the correct answer, as in the example. You have 10 seconds to choose the correct option.

Example

Listen to the woman. Which table does she want?

Woman: Excuse me. I'm looking for a round table. A round table for four people. Do you have any?

Narrator: The correct answer is C.

Number 1

Listen to the woman. What's the weather like now?

Woman: Have you seen the weather forecast for tomorrow? I hope it doesn't rain for our picnic, and it stays warm and sunny, like today.

Narrator: **Number 2**

Listen to the girl. What was Julie wearing yesterday?

Girl: I saw Julie in town yesterday. She was wearing her new jacket. Not the black one she got for her birthday, the grey one with pockets.

Narrator: **Number 3**

Listen to the woman. Where are the cups now?

Woman: James, your bedroom is in a mess. Please don't leave the cups under your bed! Either leave them in the dishwasher or wash them and put them in the cupboard.

Narrator: **Number 4**

Listen to the boy. Where is he going next week?

Boy: I'm going on a trip next week with my school. I'm quite fit, but it's going to be really hard because it's in the hills.

Narrator: **Number 5**

Listen to the man. Which cottage is he describing?

Man: The dining room is opposite the kitchen and the living room is at the end of the hall. The living room has double doors that lead out to the garden.

Narrator: **Number 6**

Listen to Emma. What's her problem?

Woman: Josh, can you call my boss and let her know I won't go to work today? I have a lot of work but I am not feeling well.

Narrator: **Number 7**

Listen to the boy. What does he have a problem with?

Boy: Hi, Jack. My laptop's not working. Fortunately, I've saved everything on a CD. I know you are busy, but could you print something for me?

Narrator: **Number 8**

Listen to the man. Where are they?

Man: Welcome, Sally, to your first day of work. I'm the manager, Mr Smith. Before you start, I'll show you where everything is.

Narrator: **Number 9**

Listen to John. What does he have to wear?

Boy: Oh, Mum, why do I have to wear a jacket and tie? Is it really necessary? I prefer something comfortable, like a T-shirt.

Narrator: **Number 10**

Listen to Sean. Which is his grandfather's house?

Boy: My grandfather lives in a nice big house. It doesn't have a garage, but it has a big garden. He parks his car there, too.

Section 2

Narrator: **Number 11**

You will hear a recording about Ann's friend. Listen to the whole recording once. Then you will hear the recording again with pauses for you to write down what you hear. Make sure you spell the words correctly.

Girl: He's quite tall. He's got dark hair. It's short and curly. His eyes are dark.

Narrator: Now listen again and write down your answer.

Girl: He's quite tall. // He's got dark hair. // It's short and curly. // His eyes are dark.

Section 3

Narrator: **Numbers 12–16**

You will hear a presentation on healthy living. First, read the notes below, then listen and complete the notes with information from the presentation. You will hear the recording twice.

Woman: Ladies and gentlemen, here are some things that doctors sometimes tell us, but we often forget about. Start in the morning with half a litre of water. The water will make you feel ready for the day. Next, make sure you always have some fruit or vegetables with you – a carrot or an apple. You can do exercise without a gym. If you have to use stairs during the day, run up them. Finally, get eight hours sleep. Too little sleep is bad for your health. Our bodies need between seven and nine hours sleep a night. Now, …

Narrator: Now listen again.

Numbers 17–21

You will hear a phone message. First, read the notes below, then listen and complete the notes with information from the message. You will hear the recording twice.

Woman: Hi, it's Judith. I'm ringing about the picnic. Let me tell you what I've got and you can ring me back if I've forgotten anything. I've made some chicken sandwiches. We had a chicken yesterday, so that was easy. I've got some eggs. Everyone will have a small packet of crisps, and for fruit I didn't know which would be better, apples or grapes. In the end, I decided that apples were easier. Talk to you soon, Beth.

Narrator: Now listen again.

That is the end of the listening section of the test. Now go on to the other sections of the test.

PTE General: Top 20 Questions

1 **How many marks are needed to pass the exam?**
To pass the exam you need a score of 50 or above.

2 **Do I have to pass each paper in order to pass the exam?**
No, each paper doesn't have a pass or fail mark. Your overall grade comes from adding your marks in both the Written and Spoken papers.

3 **Are marks taken off for wrong answers?**
No. This means that, if you are not sure, you should always try to choose the answer you think is best – you might be right.

4 **Am I allowed to use a dictionary in the exam?**
No.

5 **Generally, in the exam, if I am not sure about an answer, can I give two possible answers?**
No. If there are two answers, one of them is wrong; you will not get a mark. So you must decide on one answer to give.

6 **How many times will I hear each recording in the Listening sections?**
In Section 1, once. In Section 2, you will hear the recording twice, the second time with pauses giving you time to write down word-for-word what is heard. In Section 3, you will hear each recording twice.

7 **In Listening Section 2, what happens if I misspell a word?**
All answers need to be correctly spelt, so you will lose marks.

8 **In Listening Section 1 and Reading Section 5, what should I do if I am not sure which picture is correct?**
Check them again, there is only one correct picture. Sometimes, the pictures might look similar, but there will be some small differences that will help you find the correct answer.

9 **In Listening Section 3, should I use the words I hear in the recording?**
You can expect to hear some of the words in the recording. When you are completing sentences, you should check that the completed sentence with your answer inserted makes sense and is grammatically correct.

10 **In Listening Section 3, what happens if my answer is too long to fit in the space on the answer sheet?**
Most answers are single words, numbers or groups of two to three words. If you think the answer is longer, then it is probably incorrect.

11 **In Reading Section 6, should I write a complete sentence in answer to the questions?**
You should write only the word or words that answer the question.

12 **In Reading Section 7, what happens if I write words that are not from the article?**
The words should come from the text.

13 **In Reading Section 7, what happens if I write more than three words in a gap?**
Answers are one to three words. If you think the answer is longer, it is probably incorrect.

14 **In Writing Section 8, what happens if I don't write about all the points listed with bullet points (•)?**
You should write about all the bullet points. The examiners are looking to see if you can provide the right information and good language.

15 **In Writing Section 8, can I copy words/text from the text in Section 7?**
You can use parts of the input text in Section 7 to plan the content of your answer, but you need to use your own words and ideas as much as you can.

16 **In Writing Sections 8 and 9, what happens if I write too few or too many words?**
The word count is an important guide. It tells you how much to write when doing the task. There are tolerated ranges for each section. Your teacher will be able to guide you on these. Make sure you stay within the relevant range and use the right number of words in your answer. Plan your time so that you write about the right amount and have time to check what you have written. You will not lose score points if you stay within the tolerated word limits.

17 **What happens if I make a spelling mistake in the Writing sections?**
All spelling must be correct; spelling is one of several things that the examiner considers when deciding what mark to give you.

18 **For the Speaking paper, is it a good idea to prepare what I am going to say in Section 10?**
It is, of course, good to prepare well for the exam. But you cannot know exactly what the examiner will ask beforehand, so you must listen very carefully to the examiner and make sure you answer the questions relevantly.

19 **In Speaking Section 10, what happens if I cannot talk for one minute on my own?**
The examiner will ask you some follow-up questions to encourage you to talk more about the topic. Listen carefully to the examiner's questions before giving an answer.

20 **In Speaking Section 13, how much time will I have to prepare for the role play?**
You will have 15 seconds to prepare. Use this time to develop ideas and questions based on the test taker's card.